OBSESS *to* SUCCESS

How Building Relationships
and Focusing on the Customer Experience
Will Change the Course of Your Business

CINDY KOEBELE

ISBN 13: 978-1-63489-138-7

Library of Congress Catalog Number: 2018945721

Printed in the USA
First Printing: 2018
22   21   20   19   18   5   4   3   2   1

Cover and interior design by James Monroe Design, LLC.

Wise Ink, Inc.
807 Broadway St. NE, Suite 46
Minneapolis, MN 55413

wiseinkpub.com
To order, visit itascabooks.com or call 1-800-901-3480.
Reseller discounts available.

For my tribe –
who inspire me to lead.
You know who you are.

Special thanks to Magdalena Koebele,
who worked with me by my side through every
step of making this book a reality.

CONTENTS

Part III: Your Customers

INTRODUCTION

Never underestimate the power of a genuine connection.

Early in 2008, I went out to dinner with my husband and had a handful of business cards on me. I had founded TitleSmart a few months earlier . . . some might say the **worst** possible time to start a new company in the real estate industry! TitleSmart, Inc. is a full-service title insurance and escrow settlement services company. Are you wondering what a title insurance company is? In layman's terms, you know when you buy a house and go in, sign all those papers, and get your keys? That's us!

So, at the restaurant, I happened to see a past realtor client (Mike) from years before. For some, it would have been easier to ignore him, or to make small talk and move on. But for me, relationship building has been the key to every success in my life. So, I went up to Mike, gave him a big hug, and reconnected.

We started talking about how the real estate industry had changed (basically, the bottom fell out of the market during the housing bubble crisis). We started talking about how we were adjusting our expertise and customer bases to coincide with what was happening in the market. An example would be learning to work on distressed customers and property transactions (fore-closures and short sales, to name some examples) versus working in a flush market.

The funny thing is that Mike told me he had been thinking about me from our past working experience and that he thought I might be the one to embark on a new strategy with. Mike said I was "an expert at becoming an expert" at something new. I knew in this moment that follow-through on my part would be critical.

The following week we got coffee, and Mike told me about another realtor we would be working together with on these transactions. Those two agents became the bedrock of TitleSmart's upward trajectory. Along with being core clients, they also referred to me many others who are still in our client base today.

Good thing I always have a purse full of business cards and was ready to make a connection!

My secret is treating everyone like a potential customer. I did it in that restaurant in 2008, and I still do it every day. Treating every person like a customer hinges on building strong and genuine relationships with them—and relationships are built in the little moments. Building loyalty and rapport is a cinch when you focus on finding common ground and creating memorable experiences.

This book is about taking care of yourself and the people around you on your road to success . . . and *bringing those people with you*. If you genuinely allow yourself to care for people in your personal and professional network, the two tend to naturally collide. It's lonely at the top if you don't have your tribe around you, so support them on their paths to success, too! Sure, it feels good to achieve a dream, but it's so much sweeter to share that success with people you care about.

How to Use This Book

Putting people and relationships first makes life richer. I hope the whole world embraces that philosophy, but it starts with each of us . . . it starts with you!

This book is filled with simple, practical suggestions for creating memorable experiences with those around you and cementing relationships.

Make everything all about relationships.

Don't wait to finish the book. Start implementing tips as soon as they stick out to you. Pick out what works for you, and commit to taking action for some period of time. Not all changes will work or feel natural for everyone, but be open to trying a bunch of new approaches to business relationships. Eventually something will stick . . . and it really only takes one or two small changes to create forward momentum!

Highlight the heck out of this book, or keep a notebook nearby and write down your own ideas or reactions to the book. Then, share your thoughts with a colleague or a friend! If it could help you, your idea could probably help someone else, too.

I've built my career on a special mix of strong relationships and big leaps of faith. I've had my share of luck, but I've had plenty of unlucky times too—so I credit my current business to being bold and trusting the communities I've created around me.

I can't define success for you. I can't tell you what salary to aim for, or what size house to dream about—only you know what will fulfill you emotionally and physically. What I can tell you is that you will only feel truly successful when you focus on the people and goals that matter most to *you*.

Take stock of how satisfied you feel in your personal life and your career—where do you spend your time, and where do you *wish* you were spending your time?

Born to Be an Entrepreneur

By the time I was 9 or 10, I was already working in my parents' record store. Both of my parents worked, and my siblings and I were expected to cook and clean for ourselves. By age 16, I was assistant-managing a restaurant, and I was pouring my energy into my work. I was bullied at school, but when I got to the restaurant each day, I dove in fully. That was the genesis of my strategy to focus on what I can control when I'm faced with negativity.

That philosophy was the seed of my decision to start my own business in 2007. I was happy at my job, but I had a million ideas for improving the customer experience. My bosses and I did not see eye to eye, and I realized I had peaked at that company . . . I wasn't going to get any more of the creative freedom that I craved.

So I took a deep breath, and in the face of negativity at that job, I took a huge risk and bet on myself. I quit my job and started my own company. I was at a point in my life where things were not progressing financially.

Actually, I was poor as a church mouse. So I really had nothing to lose in that area. I was totally house-poor and my income was not climbing. I was bursting with ideas and had an employer who would not listen to any of my ideas or suggestions. Perhaps I was naïve, as I didn't realize at the time that failing was an option. I specifically remember sitting at a table with our two staff members and telling them, "We must will this company into being."

I was a single mom with two little kids, but was fortunate enough to have my parents to help me while I worked the long, strenuous hours starting my new business. I agree, it was a huge risk!

It was seemingly the exact wrong time to start a new company in the real estate industry. Remember the end of 2007? Looking back, I am amazed that I had the balls to do it. But I'm grateful for the strength inside me, and *for the people around me*. I give so much credit to my tribe. I had cultivated relationships for years, and they paid dividends when I needed support most. Who would support you in a time of change?

Whenever people ask me how I built this business, I look at them and say, **"One relationship at a time."**

A Genuine Connection . . .

I can't say this enough: be transparent, genuine, and honest in your relationships. If you can build trust in those around you, you will create ripple effects that carry your good name out further than you can imagine.

No good work happens alone, and no single relationship will keep a company afloat indefinitely. Connections and relationships are abundant, which means business is abundant!

Part I:
You

CHAPTER 1:

The Basics of Building Relationships

In 2008, my business was barely chugging along. Let me tell you about Max. Remember the first story I told you about, meeting my customer Mike in the restaurant? From that encounter spun another relationship with my all-time best client.

Mike connected me with Max to work with us on those short sales and foreclosures. As I mentioned earlier, things had shifted and those of us in the industry needed to shift as well if we wanted to stay in the business. This was a time when only the strategic and flexible would survive.

I started talking with Max over the phone—we hadn't met in person yet. The funny thing is, when we first started working together he was a little leery; he'd previously worked with and had a long-term relationship with another real-estate closer. I was nervous. I didn't want to blow this. I wanted to make sure that he liked me, because in this tough market every client was critical. Our first face-to-face contact was at a closing. I walked in the room and introduced myself. There was an immediate professional chemistry and confidence between us which led to our building the best short sale process I have seen to this day. We literally built our systems and process together and learned from each other, which laid the relationship foundation that we maintain today.

One relationship can change the course of your business—trust in the power of connections.

Tips by Cindy:

- **Start conversations.** You never know who you might run into. Be ready!

- **Have business cards.** Make sure they are up to date . . . and hand them out! When you receive someone else's card, write a note on it to yourself to remember that connection.

Relationships Are Built Everywhere

I own my company and am intimately invested in its success, so wherever I am, I spread the word about my business as if my life depends on it (because it does!). And when I say wherever, I mean *wherever.*

Whenever I go into an escrow closing with customers, I fully expect to make a new connection that could produce more business. Throughout a typical business day, I keep my name badge on and am always ready to hand out a business card or a branded pen. When I'm at the gas station or the pharmacy, I'm always chatting with the people around me—sometimes we just make a connection. Oftentimes, my kids get embarrassed and ask me why I have to chat with everybody. I tell them you just never know how you can affect someone's day by caring and giving them some attention. For example, what about that lonely person who feels completely invisible in life? What kind of impact could you have by just having a simple conversation that can be a total game changer for this person? I've gotten countless clients or referrals just by mentioning my work in unexpected conversations and handing them a business card!

Seven years ago, I was at a picture-taking gathering for my stepdaughter's prom. I was dressed down in a sweatshirt and jeans (my genuine self!), but remember: I'm always working to be an advocate for my business. My stepdaughter's date's mom, Julie, mentioned that she owned a real estate brokerage, and we immediately began talking about the industry and how we could work together in the future!

Here's how it shook down: my husband loudly exclaimed, "Hey! My wife owns a title company!" Of course I was embarrassed and downplayed things. Subsequently, Julie started talking about her company and mentioned that she already had a closer with another title company she was committed to. I told her that if she ever needed a backup, she should give me a call. I also invited her to stop by our office to see it and have some gourmet coffee and a cookie. She did! And we have been working together ever since! She also owns her real estate brokerage and connected me to all of her agents, so now I close for many of them too. She has since become a top client and a really close friend. I didn't let the fact that I was out of "work mode" stop me from making that critical connection, but I kept it genuine and not overbearing. I didn't go in for the kill. Instead, I planted the seed and watered it for when the opportunity might present itself.

I have learned that personal connections can transition into business relationships and vice versa. Every connection, friendship, or encounter could lead to a new customer.

Tips by Cindy:

- **Roll out the red carpet.** Make your clients, customers, and vendors feel special. Give them your company's five-star treatment.

- **Wear a name badge.** You never know who will notice your name badge—even if they don't mention it then, potential customers will remember it.

- **Follow up on connections.** Most people meet at an event or get handed a business card and never think about that connection again. Be the exception to that rule with a quick note *and* a connection on social media to nurture the relationship.

How Do I Build Relationships?

I'm not just talking about collecting casual professional acquaintances. Real benefits come from real connections: friends help friends. Here are some of the keys I've found to turn encounters into relationships and acquaintances into meaningful connections.

Communication

Communication is the root of building relationships, especially when meeting someone in person. Your words, actions, and body language tell everyone what they need to know about you. So I'll only tell you once: mean what you say and say what you mean. Be authentic. Be clear. No B.S.

Face-to-Facing:

Talk to your connections like you care about them, and like they are your equal.

- Be friendly and approachable.

- No industry jargon.

- Be *there*. Really listen to them, and be **in the moment**.

Digital Facing:

Also, consider your accessibility. In this day and age, when you or your staff are unreachable, chances are you've got a competitor who *is* available. What is your email response time? You can beat out the competition with response time alone: it conveys how important the relationship is to you. That said, your responses must still be genuine, thought-out, and appropriately detailed!

From time to time, when customers reach out to me for a quote for a closing, I know they are shopping other title company services. When they end up choosing my company, I ask what the deciding factor was for them. Typically the answer is that I responded quicker than anyone else and the customer felt that we connected and built trust.

I own my own business, so I'm dedicated to working 24/7. I'm also a mom and a wife, so I strive to balance my emails and phone calls with being truly present for my family. My strategy is quick and short responses to confirm that I'm in the loop. If I'm at my son's hockey game and see a few emails come through, I respond with something as easy as, "You got it," or "Yes, I'll get back to you in the A.M.!" Or a big smiley emoticon. Naturally, I can address the matter further and in more detail when I am back at my desk in "work mode."

A reply like that takes the pressure off my client or employee without absorbing my attention or hijacking my evening. Demonstrating that I'm invested in their concerns requires little effort and makes a huge impact. So many times, I get the response "Thank you for the quick reply!" just because I wrote them a ten-second note. How hard was that?

Tips by Cindy:

- **Manage your emails.** Even just a confirmation saying you got a request ("I'm on it!") allows the sender to stop worrying about it—it's on your plate now!

- **Stay in touch.** Even reaching out because you haven't heard from a client, a vendor, or a friend in a while will let them know that they are on your priority list.

Personal Attention

Have you ever been around someone who makes you feel like you are the only person in the room? That's true personal attention. Expert relationship builders put huge value on one-on-one interactions, and they say hi to both bigwigs and new kids.

A few years ago, I met a guy who did high-level financial management for businesses. He invested personal attention in order to create a long-term relationship. He invited me to professional lunches, dropped off books that were relevant to a conversation we had, and sent inspirational notes. Over time, we just became friends—and last year, I swapped out one of my vendors just so I could do business with him. Friends help friends.

Keep track of each connection:

- **Know names.** This is tough! I still struggle with it after years of making it my mantra, but I know nothing feels better than when someone acknowledges you by name.

- **Know specifics**. Do whatever helps to remember specifics about your last interaction or their needs. Keep notes on the back of their business card, or in their contact entry in your phone.

- **Treat it like a courtship**. Just like a romantic relationship, budding professional relationships require courting: keep track of the relationship and put in the energy it needs to grow! I like to send handwritten notes and cards, put little notes on people's computer monitor or work station, and send random check-in emails and texts; just small gestures to make sure people know I am thinking about them. Sometimes I like to stay after hours and play "Santa Claus" with inspirational notes for our staff to find in the morning.

Tips by Cindy:

- **Send thank-you cards.** Thank everyone! Thank your vendor partners, thank your clients, and thank your staff. Everyone contributes to a job well done! Again, everyone is a customer.

- **Send other cards.** Don't underestimate the power of a handwritten note. Cards for birthdays, kids' graduations, bereavement, or congratulations are always appropriate and impactful. Think about how receiving a card makes you feel. I know I love getting a little personal card in the mail or finding one on my desk left by someone.

Always Put Your Best Foot Forward

Your industry should be like the bar *Cheers*: it's where everybody knows your name! Spread your name, spread your brand, and ensure that your reputation is polished and professional. I am not shoving it down their throat—*it's just a general narrative that I am the brand, and the brand is me.* My brand reflects positive energy and concepts, and seriously, nobody minds this.

It is a feel-good message that anybody could get behind. It's like positive, feel-good everything . . . oh, and by the way, we are a title company!

Home ownership is considered the American dream and most people are at some point going to buy a house. The process is very intimidating and scary. Part of my branding message is that closing on your house should be fun!

Everyone I know thinks of me when they think of the title industry. For all things related to title and home ownership, I am their person. I get questions from **everybody** about **everything** real estate. Whether it pertains to me or not, I am the contact, the resource, the expert. Because of that, I refer a lot of business to my friends and colleagues in the real estate world. And referring business creates loyalty . . . which creates more business! Here are some ways to make sure people are thinking of you when they think of your industry.

Business Cards

I can't tell you how many working professionals (sales people especially) do not carry a stash of their business cards

with them or do not update their card when their information changes. These are—pardon me for saying so—the stupidest mistakes I've ever witnessed. People say it all the time: "I don't have any cards on me right now," or, "Sorry, I crossed out my old number and wrote in my new one." *What?!* Your business depends on connections, but you don't have your main sales tool in your pocket, or it's been scribbled on as if you're a high-schooler? Sloppy or non-existent business cards tell the customer you half-ass your networking, and who could blame them for assuming you half-ass your business?

And *before you say the business card is dead*—I assure you it is not. For instance, I have a book full of business cards in my office. Whenever I get a card from a new connection, I take it back to my office and immediately find its owner on social networks. That card sits right in front of my computer until I make that connection. Once I have made the connection, I put that card into my book so that I can hand it out if I refer that person to a future friend, client, or vendor. And I do this with *every* business card I collect.

I expect my closers (customer reps) to have 25-50 cards with them at all times, because I too expect them to sieze the moment.

Tips by Cindy:

- **Never show up empty-handed.** Whether it's branded swag like pens or coffee mugs, treats, or personalized gifts, I like to always bring some sort of trinket to every current or potential customer interaction. My customers are used to it and they know I usually never show up empty-handed, whether it's just a piece of candy or a special pen. Remember—*everyone* is a customer and people love feeling special!

Online Presence

These days, you don't have a choice in social media: you've got to *do it, and do it well.* Social networks have made it easier than ever to make connections, but just like in person, you have to stand out. Your social media pages must be:

- **Up to date**. Nothing is worse than when I go to look someone up and they have information from three companies ago. Seriously?

- **Relevant**. Same as above. Also, make sure your branding and experience actually match what you do.

- **Active**. An inactive profile says "lazy." How hard is it to update information from time to time? If I don't see that you are active, chances are I am not reaching out to you as I'm worried my message will go to an old, inactive, moldy email in no man's land.

Consider Your Online Presence. Do You Follow These Golden Rules?

- **Put others' wants and needs before your own.** Don't be that person who sends a canned InMail request to a random LinkedIn connection . . . I personally delete *all* of these, and I'm sure everyone else does too! Don't immediately ask to meet up . . . I don't have time for coffee with my staff, family, or friends, let alone a stranger! Instead, let your online presence be the seeds of the relationship: interact with their interesting and relevant content and post your own. This technique, rather than attacking, attracts people to your content to interact. The goal is to establish a courtship—in this case, we are flirting toward a courtship.

- **Be genuine.** Generic comments on Facebook, Instagram, and Twitter have no power—except for negative power if they start reading as spam. Social media is meant for conversations, so craft genuine comments when you have something positive to add.

- **Engage.** Do so not only on business topics, but also their personal posts (if you are connected on a personal site). Look for what you two have in common. **Remember, it is a courtship.** Small and frequent connections equal flirting equals courting. Be memorable, be real, and be fun.

Tips by Cindy:

- **Manage social media.** You can build relationships and never leave your desk or couch! Keep your information up to date. Engage with your customers' content through likes, shares, and comments to connect on a personal level. Remember that social media is free, which makes this even more fun to use.

- **Let your personality shine.** Identify which part of your personality lends itself best to confidence and positivity—and embrace that when forming bonds with people!

Say Yes

A few years ago, I guest-hosted a real estate radio hour in our metro area. I first heard about the opportunity from one of my lender customers, and without knowing any details, I cheered, "I'm in!" While it wasn't a direct business referral, I already understood the importance of breaking into a new marketing space, both personally and for my company.

I connected immediately with the show owner—we understood the impact that this guest spot could have on both of our businesses. I could barely breathe before the first show, I was so excited! I've stayed close with the program, recording commercial spots, becoming a show sponsor, and appearing as a guest on the show a few times a year. Every one of those interactions is full of potential new clients . . . in just the first three years of the relationship with the program, I picked up countless new customers and formed long-lasting referral relationships. Seize opportunities when they come along, and chase your positive gut feelings—every interaction has the potential for a new relationship or referral.

CHAPTER 2:

Get Organized

I'm constantly being asked, "How do you do it all?" My answer:

I do everything with a passion as if my life depends on it—and that requires organization. Since I obsess to success, I organize my time, my to-do lists, my team, and my long-term goals.

Organization is a skill that needs to be intentional and practiced—like yoga!

People are reluctant to change their habits, but my philosophy is that we like what we are used to . . . so make the change, take a few days to get used to it, and soon it will be your new favorite. I'm constantly joking around with people about my thoughts on this. Sometimes they look at me, confused, as they mull it over before saying to me, "Oh yeah, I get it now, good point."

The 1440 (Minutes)

We all have 1,440 minutes in a day. How you manage those minutes and where you spend them

determines how productive and efficient you are that day. How well do you manage those minutes right now? Are you making conscious choices about how you spend

that time? Are you saying yes to too many commitments or invitations?

When someone asks you if you've got a minute, make sure you do! (You can always remind them that one minute is all you have!) **Every yes is no to something else.**

Balancing success at work and health in your personal life is a hard job and can leave you feeling overwhelmed or exhausted. I fell in love with this whole concept after reading Hank Reardon's *Time Management 2.0*.

If you are balancing your work schedule with your personal schedule, think about how many social obligations you participate in each week, or how many evenings you spend meeting clients. If you don't really want to go to that extra happy hour, don't! I get invited to lots of what I call time intensive (or time sucker) events. Even though they sound fun and I appreciate that they thought of me, I cannot possibly go to them all, so I politely decline and say, "I'm sorry that I can't make this." Sometimes I just say point-blank, "Unfortunately, every yes is a no to something else, so I have to say no to this one." People get it and love an honest answer. What can you give up to make your life better?

It's easy to blame outside pressures for our inefficiencies at work, but your productivity is a result of choices you make, consciously or not. If you're not satisfied with your routine, reorganize it!

Ask yourself:

- Am I overcommitting or overbooking my calendar?

- Am I leaving enough time to get things done?

- What can I say no to?

Reorganize Your Organization

I know, I know . . . how confusing does that sound? *Reorganize your organization?* But I promise: your systems can always be improved. For example, once a year I love to go through and revamp my systems. I reorganize my file drawers, relabel my folders, purge old items, and clean my entire office. It's like changing your room around— freshen it up! Then, after a few days of adjustment, I'm back in my "zone."

I first developed this habit when I lived in Switzerland for two years and studied German. Every day after class, I would reorganize my notes and recopy them in a visual system to enable me to recall the information easier. Every month or two I would take full stock of what I had learned. I sure learned German faster because of those reviews—but I also set up a valuable routine for myself.

I am always looking for a better way to organize to make my systems faster and more efficient. By taking the time to reorganize my organization, I do my job better for my staff and my customers.

Tips by Cindy:

- **Tidy up.** Clean up your workspace and keep it that way. Organization and neatness send the message that you've got your act together. Messy piles on your desk will make your coworkers and customers think, "Is my stuff in there?" Yikes! You don't want your customers thinking, "What a dump!"

- **Personalize the space.** As a balance to neatness, make sure that your office and the workplace have personality! Hang art that you love which reflects the atmosphere of your organization. Post congratulatory notes and team photos. *No bland pictures of grass! Move in and stay for a while!*

Short Term

Since I like to produce things and check things off my list, I like the baby-steps concept: lots of short things add up to long things, and a lot of little things add up to big things. I'll discuss this more later in the chapter. These are specific habits you can start forming today:

- **Say no.** Remember 1,440: when your 1,440 minutes in each day are precious, saying yes to a work commitment means saying no to something else. We can't be everything for everyone every day; that just isn't productive. If you are truly giving it your all but your to-do list is never getting shorter or you feel yourself falling short, identify what you can say no to. This might mean turning down the request entirely, delegating to someone else, or simply asking for help. Of course, you shouldn't be saying no if saying no is going to get you fired!

- **Write it down.** Make notes and lists however works for you—on your phone, in a notebook, in a voice memo, on sticky notes . . . whatever!

The Art of the Steno Pad

With all the distractions in today's world, finding a way to finish your to-do list can sometimes feel like a daunting task. When people are feeling overwhelmed, they often look to others to find an organizational method to help them stay on task. There are so many different ways to keep yourself organized out there, and trust me, I have tried them all! And of all the things I have tried, there is one that has stood the test of time: the steno pad.

Now, you might be thinking, "What? Of all the tools, programs, and apps available, you use a notebook? How is this going to revolutionize the way I keep myself organized?" My answer is "KISS": Keep It Simple, Stupid! Trust Albert Einstein and many other geniuses who used this concept over the course of history.

In all seriousness, organizing your life *should* be simple. You shouldn't have to learn a new program or make things more complicated than they have to be. Find a clean system that works for you and run with it.

I like to keep a steno pad on my desk, and each morning I write down a quick list of things I need to complete right away. I always try to tackle the most diffi-cult or intimidating task first, then order the rest based on priority. Throughout the day, I'm adding things I can't forget to address. When my page gets too full or messy, I flip it over, start a new clean page, and carry over what I haven't gotten to. My goal is to not leave the office until everything on my steno pad is complete. Slightly obsessive? Maybe! Do I go through tons of steno pads? Definitely! But hey, it works for me . . . and guess what? I have my whole office using them. And I can't lie, there is nothing more satisfying than looking at my notebook, seeing all my completed tasks, and flipping over to a clean page. Ahhhh!

The Art of the Checkbox

The other day I was helping my son with his small business. I was giving him a list of things to do when I noticed something peculiar. I looked down at his paper to realize he was drawing small boxes next to each item on his to-do list. I immediately exclaimed, "Hey! I

do that too!" I couldn't believe that without realizing it, people around me were catching onto the Art of the Check Box when putting together their checklist.

Now, you might be asking yourself, "What the heck is the 'Art of the Check Box'?" Let me break it down for you: For years, I have been drawing small boxes next to all the items on my to-do list. When I give a to-do list to an employee, I often hand them a hand-written list with little boxes. Then, when I complete something on my checklist, I check off the box next to the item. I literally get to "check" it off my list!

These checkboxes have not only slowly become a part of my everyday life, but have also spread to my staff. I will look around the office and see that many of my staff members use these checkboxes every day on their own to-do lists! It has become so popular that we even designed notepads for our closing rooms with the checkbox next to each line. During a closing, our clients love that they have a convenient place to write down last-minute items that come up. They can leave with their checklist, mark off each box when the task is complete, and feel the same sense of satisfaction that my staff and I do.

Let me tell you, there is *nothing* more gratifying than checking off those little boxes. Just like my steno pad, these check boxes have become a staple in how I keep myself organized throughout the day. Will these change your life? Maybe. Are they fun, and do they make you feel accomplished? Heck yeah! Sometimes it really is the little things that make the big difference.

Long Term

These are mindset shifts; with dedication, these mindsets can become healthy habits.

- **Set boundaries**. Know your limits both personally and professionally. Maybe you want to be home in time for dinner with the family every night. Block off that time on your calendar, and communicate that boundary at work. Allowing yourself boundaries helps you remain motivated and on-task in your career, instead of getting overstretched.

- **Know when to change the plan**. Kids get sick, cars break down, and deadlines get moved. It just happens. Know when to call your baby-sitter and spend an evening working late, or ask for help from your team when something unexpected happens at home. It's okay to adapt, shift your attention, and ask for help.

We all make time for what we really want or need to do. You know that if those shoes are on sale at Macy's and the sale ends today, no matter how busy you are, you will figure out a time to stop by!

You have full control over your days and how you spend them. Go get organized.

The Art of "Touch It Once"

When I first read about the "Touch It Once" principle in Hank Reardon's *Time Management 2.0*, it was a game changer. I apply it to my email practice every day—and to many other areas of my life.

Every email in your inbox should fall into one of three categories:

1. Fast: Respond immediately and quickly, file it, or delete it.

2. Delegate: Forward to someone else.

3. Slow: Skip it entirely (until you have time to go back and apply #1 or #2).

The "Touch It Once" principle is another skill that requires practice (remember, like yoga?). Develop this skill over time so you can remind yourself to practice it when you go into email overload. The goal is to achieve a clean email inbox without pouring in too much time. It drives me absolutely crazy to have emails in my inbox that are unaddressed, but also, reading an email two, three, or four times sucks up minutes in my 1,440! "Touch It Once" means I decide immediately whether I can eliminate that email from my to-do list, or need to skip it until later when I have time to address it.

Think about it: *"Touch It Once" can work in many other areas of your life. I use it when I'm paying my bills—I either pay a bill quickly or put it in my bill folder until I have time to dive in! I also use it when I'm clearing off the table after dinner—dishes should go straight to the dishwasher instead of sitting on the counter!*

Tips by Cindy:

- **Use the tools.** Set automatic rules for certain senders or categorize your emails by color. Figure out what works for you!

- **Do your crappiest task first.** The top of your steno pad should list the one thing you don't want to do, but need to do. Do this first and get it out of the way! *Whew*! And *never* leave something like that on your to-do list when you go home for the weekend . . . weekend ruined.

- **Delegate.** If you have a team, they're there for a reason. I often joke with my team and say, "If I have to do it myself, I want your paycheck too!" Spend time teaching people to help you be more productive in your job, and then give them opportunities to grow!

- **Limit distractions.** If you aren't using your cell phone to work, put it away! If I ignore distractions during the day, I find that I go home earlier to do the things I want to do—not just because I was more efficient, but because I am excited about the rewards of doing little things like catching up on social media.

CHAPTER 3:
Get Positive

One of my clearest memories of starting TitleSmart comes from January of 2008. I looked through my file rack, and it was mostly empty. *Holy shit . . . I need some business.* It was the depth of the housing crisis, and I knew that my business partner and I had no choice but to **will** the company into being. By "**will** it into being" I mean I needed to believe beyond the shadow of a doubt that the business would succeed, and not allow any negative thought to deter or distract me from making that happen. After some soul-searching, I realized that there was no way I could manifest success without positivity: about the work, about the future, and about my choice to walk this uncertain path.

I decided to choose **intentional positivity**, meaning that no matter what, I would focus only on positive thoughts of growth and success. It felt almost like a superstition—but I had to believe it would work. I didn't have any other choice. Remember the dinner I had with my husband that I mentioned in Chapter 1? That was a night when prospects seemed particularly bleak . . . but I told myself, "I am going to meet someone tonight and make a connection." And sure enough, I saw my old client Mike and the rest is history. Our little interaction was the spark that lit the fire of success under TitleSmart. I believe that would never have happened if I hadn't been focusing on positivity and looking for opportunity in the face of seemingly certain failure.

I should stop right here and say: I love my job. I love the work I do, I love the people I work with, and succeeding in my career makes me feel fulfilled. *Of course* it's easier to commit to positivity if you love the foundations of your work. That said, **intentional positivity can make your life easier even if you don't love what you're doing**. Train yourself to be as positive as you can about whatever you are involved in—and if that feels impossible, consider chasing what would really make you happy! Some of the things I do are reading positive and empowering books, listening to inspirational podcasts, and cutting out complaining about anything and anyone in general. (That helps no one!) I also have a daily positive affirmations desk calendar and I will often rip out the pages and tape them to other people's office doors and computers to build the positive momentum. One of my absolute favorite positive things is the daily emails you can sign up for from TUT.com, "Notes from the Universe."

Tips by Cindy:

- **When you feel your worst, dress your best.** When you feel your worst, put on something that makes you feel great. Wear a full suit the day you come back from vacation, or your favorite heels to an intimidating meeting. Even if you feel like crap, dressing in something you really like can change the energy of your day and your attitude.

Positivity Is Contagious

I don't know about you, but I would rather work in a fun, upbeat environment than a crabby one. People will mirror the tone of the office. Translation: monkey see, monkey do. Being around positive people is contagious.

Tips by Cindy:

- **Email positively.** The person on the other end of your email can feel your energy. I love exclamation points and smiley faces: they're my way of telling my client that I am dedicated to taking care of their needs. I want my client to know that I'm excited—I'm smiling while typing! If you're not a smiley face person, think about how you can still convey an upbeat tone in your emails.

- **Get your head in the game.** If you're feeling off, change your energy by changing your vibe. I often take deep breaths, shake my head around, and do some Rocky punches. This is my version of mental preparation—don't knock it 'till you try it!

- **Lift those eyebrows.** Lifting your eyebrows naturally

forms your face into a more enthusiastic, lively expression—it sets a trend that your inflection usually follows.

- **Don't gossip.** Avoid trash talk about staff members, competitors, and your customers. What comes out of your mouth can and will spread like wildfire through your office . . . and sometimes, the industry.

Don't Give Up

Be persistent! I started TitleSmart in the thick of a recession . . . if that doesn't scream perseverance, then I don't know what does. Don't give up on positivity. Even after a really negative day, when you can't keep positivity at the top of your mind, *start again tomorrow*. There is nothing to lose by trying again. Just like exercise or training a puppy, you won't see progress tomorrow, but you will see it over time.

Sometimes It's Hard

There are just "those days" and "those weeks" where it feels like nothing goes right and you're in a funk. Remember in the spirit of obsession, try some of these for success:

- **Be honest with yourself and others** and make a plan of action to reboot. I like to reboot by going shopping, binge-watching a show, or reading a book that completely takes me out of my daily routine and lets me recharge my batteries.

- **Stand up for yourself.** If you've been wronged, take steps to make it right—but don't let your negativity lead to pettiness or vengeance.

- **Get through the day. Allow yourself to process and start fresh the next day.** Don't let your bad mood drain the energy from other people's days.

- **Definitely don't get absorbed in gossip or drama.** You're probably susceptible to that when you're already feeling low. For me, the art of distraction helps keep my blinders up so I can focus on positive energy. Translation = keep busy!

CHAPTER 4:
Monkey See, Monkey Do

I don't expect my employees, or anyone I rely on, to do anything that I wouldn't do myself. That's my firm philosophy. I want people to feel supported and inspired by my actions, to feel equal  in talent and value, and to have a clear example to follow.

A week before writing this, I had a group of employees in my office. One of them said, "It's just a lot of work to keep up with clients' and vendors' lives." I immediately pulled open a file drawer in my desk—it's stuffed with cards. I told them, "These are bereavement cards, congratulations cards, and get well cards. I pay attention to what my friends, family, and client base are doing . . . and *I send a lot of cards.*"

Showing others what works for me is an easy way to set the example and inspire them to find their own niche. My technique of sending cards is an easy way to keep in touch with people who are important to my work and my life. I don't expect every one of those employees who sat in my office that day to keep a stash of greeting cards in their desk, but I'm confident that they will find their own ways of connecting after seeing concrete proof that I walk the walk.

Momentum Is Contagious

Momentum, which is a driving force, almost always comes from the top of an organization. As a leader, your obsessive attitude and energy are contagious. Plus, it's easier for clients and vendors to identify with a company's mission through a real, live person than a logo.

I am a sleeve roller-upper. I never hesitate to roll up my sleeves when needed and get down and dirty with my staff. Getting busy with others creates that excitement to push forward and get things done: momentum.

I've never been the earliest riser. If I could, I would work from 10 A.M. to 7 P.M. But I know that I can't set that example for my staff . . . so I make sure I'm in the office early, no matter what! I can only imagine how much I'd grumble if I had to watch my boss float in at any old time of day, and I strive to never be a hypocrite. The momentum of others then in turn drives me to get up and get in early.

I never want any employee to go home and say, "She thinks her time is more valuable than mine." I never want any employee to whisper in the lunchroom, "She thinks that the basic rules of conduct and ethics don't apply to her." In a successful business, you must perform if you expect your team to perform. You have to lead the staff by example and get into the office early, or come in during a snowstorm, or show up to the meeting even when you don't feel 100 percent. If I'm the first person in the office that day, I will start the coffee. When we moved our office location, I packed my own office. I like to get the job done alongside my team.

It strengthens your business's culture when you choose to be its living, breathing example every day. And if you're not the boss, you never know; someday you might be. Take time now to practice for your future.

Tips by Cindy:

- **Eat with your co-workers.** This gives you a chance to get to know your team better, especially new employees.

- **Have an open-door policy.** I like to keep an open-door policy with staff and clients so they know they can stop in to talk to me when they need to—of course, I set boundaries for the time of the day!

- **Participate.** I make it a point to be at company events or staff outings, and even non-work events that staff and clients invite me to. That said, I adhere to my "saying yes is a no to something else" philosophy!

- **Greet co-workers by name.** Don't be a grouch! If you need coffee before you talk to people, then get that coffee in you before you get in the office—set an energetic example for your employees throughout the day.

But I'm Not a Manager

Every task is valuable. Do everything with a passion. If you are making a copy, it better be the best damn copy you have ever made! A few years ago I was inspired by this thought process after reading Bethenny Frankel's *A Place of Yes*. Every employee in every position has the potential to lead. Look around you: no matter what position you hold, there will most likely be someone who is learning from you. No matter what the position, **no task is too small.** Be the kind of leader that you would follow. Be the type of person who inspires others to be obsessed . . . I mean their best.

Support your company's brand and culture, no matter what your pay grade. If you are passionate about your workplace, spread that news! If you love your company's digital innovations, post about those on LinkedIn, Facebook, or Instagram. Your passion will shine through for clients and customers . . . *and* for your fellow coworkers. It may even create a future opportunity for you—you never know! I know what you're thinking: *This sounds like it is helping my employer, not me.* My point is, everything comes around full-circle. If you want to make a change or experience growth, you have to be **all in** to get to that next level. You never know who is noticing the impact you are having and what type of opportunities will be available to you.

Tips by Cindy:

- **Follow the rules like everyone else.**
  Nothing makes team members feel jaded or reduces loyalty like a leader or coworker appearing above the law. For example, I don't reserve a space for myself at the front of the parking lot—I park where the employees do. Well geez, I don't think I'm the Queen of England, for God's sakes! Plus, walking is good for me!

If Everyone Is Successful, Everyone Is Successful

Expending your own energy to set an example for others is never a waste. Demonstrating positive progress in the business is part of being a great leader in any role . . . so "spreading the love" is actually success in and of itself!

I believe in every piece of advice and direction I give. You read earlier about relationship building—I'm serious about it! A few months ago, a gal who works for me lost someone close to her, and I knew what she was going through. I made sure that every day on my steno pad checkbox to-do list, I wrote her name down. At the end of the day when I was clearing off my desk, I'd reach out to her. Whether it was a short text, an email, or even just sending a photo I knew she'd like, I wanted to make her feel supported. In turn, she'll pass that support on to other coworkers and clients. I firmly believe in genuine connections as a foundation for success in business . . . and that's not just lip service.

Do you notice that a lot of this has to do with positivity? Positivity is my single most significant predictor of company success: if leaders, employees, and clients feel positive (and determined to stay positive) about the business, you can bet it will succeed. During the real estate slow season, it's common for clients to come into my office a little mopey. They complain about the market and start telling me about the future economic predictions (zzzz). I tell them to stop focusing on the negativity, and encourage them to take a step toward making a new connection. By the time they leave my office, the client is inevitably excited!

What Would **You** Want in a Leader?

Consider that question seriously. How many bosses have you loved? Hated? What behaviors set them apart? Take time to consider how you mirror leaders' styles, and reflect on what habits you like and don't like. Be honest with yourself. No one is asking you but you!

Lead Through Change

From a business owner's perspective, in 2015, the mortgage and title industry underwent some form and compliance changes that truly shook up the real estate industry. I made it crystal clear to my customers and staff that we were ready for the change and would lead the way for them so they could relax and trust us. I made it a priority to go to every compliance course and train all my staff to make sure we were 100 percent ready to get our clients through the change as smooth as silk. Having that level of expertise immediately created the narrative that TitleSmart was the company "in the know."

From an employee perspective, we recently had an employee who took the lead and was able to spearhead a new product and process to better protect our company from cybercrime. He presented his idea to me; I loved it and let him run with it, and now he has gotten our staff on board and excited. Something that was daunting for our industry has created an incredible opportunity for growth for someone who was willing to embrace it.

Tips by Cindy:

- **Face the change head-on**. Don't fight it, do the research, and implement your processes immediately. You're going to have to deal with it anyway. Don't go kicking and screaming.

- **Become the expert**. Learn everything you can: research, take classes, and then teach others.

- **Don't freak out.** Take a deep breath and trust that you've got this.

- **Communicate.** Keep clients and staff in the know. I send emails to clients and staff explaining company or industry changes. People want info right from the source!

Use change as a competitive advantage. The faster and more adeptly you embrace technology, trends, and industry shifts, the more firmly you will place yourself at the head of the pack. Remember, we like what we are used to. When you make a change, it feels uncomfortable at first, but as soon as you get used to it, you like it! It's on you to encourage your team to face change with optimism . . . lead with positivity.

Part II:
Your Team

CHAPTER 5:
Loyalty

People are always asking me to identify my biggest challenge when it comes to growing my business, and my answer is always the same: **finding and attracting talented staff members who possess the values and work ethic necessary to meet our high service expectations.** (I call them our "Smarties" because they are obsessed about the customer experience.) But you know what I don't have an issue with? *Keeping those employees.*

At TitleSmart, we have nailed employee retention—or, as I think of it, employee loyalty. I use empowerment, respect, and a clear path into the future to encourage loyalty, and boy is it effective! I don't have to crack any whip because I am good to them, and so they are good to me.

Tips by Cindy:

- **Get excited about the little things.** I like to celebrate the little things and the big things with my staff. Birthdays, big events, newborn babies, career milestones; any excuse to team build. Of course, this relates to positivity and showing appreciation.

Loyalty Trickles Down

Employees who are loyal to the business will work harder to support the business. Their hard work impacts customers, who end up with a top-notch experience—and that positive experience leads to repeat business and word-of-mouth recommendations. Loyal employees lead to loyal customers, who lead to more customers and stronger applicants for open positions. No matter what you think of trickle-down economics, **trickle-down loyalty** is a tried-and-true concept. Remember hearing "Treat people they way you would like to be treated," or "Do unto others as you would have them do unto you," or "What goes around comes around"? There is a reason these sayings have stood the test of time: when you are loyal to someone, they will be loyal to you—well, most of the time.

I started TitleSmart with my sister as well as a friend who came to work with us at our new business, and the three of us still operate as a team to move the company forward. We've set the example of loyalty, making it easier for our team and customers to follow suit.

And I mean it when I say trickle-down loyalty is real: my employees love TitleSmart so much that they frequently recruit their family members and friends to work with them. Over the years we have had many families represented at TitleSmart who have had at least two (and in some cases three) family members working at the company in some capacity. That's more than 20 percent of our staff who have referred TitleSmart as a great place to work to their closest loved ones, which I think of as a very high compliment.

You might be wondering: why would employees be so loyal? Owning a company has a lot of risk factors and operational responsibilities; most people don't care to open their own business, or want to deal with that headache. They just want a stable job, some great benefits, and family time. Honestly, there are days when I walk through the halls and think to myself, "Wow! This is a serious business and my name is signed to a lot of things!" Try sleeping with all *that* on your mind. I am committed to *that*. They are committed to *me*. This is the trickle-down.

Tips by Cindy:

- **Set the example.** I demonstrate my loyalty to my staff through both rewards and relationship-building . . . and they mirror that.

Respect Your Team

I work hard to clearly communicate to my employees that I respect their time and effort. I do this by rewarding their work (check out Chapter 7), but also by offering them challenging projects. I make sure that my employees know that it is a compliment from me to challenge them—it means I see potential and strength in their work ethic.

Back in 2009, I hired a part-time assistant as my business was growing. She was sharp as a tack and impressed me immediately, and I made sure to let her know that I saw her potential. Step by step, she continued to learn and work her way up to become my operations manager and right-hand person. Oftentimes she would still mention to me that she could not believe how far she had come. It was clear that hard work builds to opportunity.

Tips by Cindy:

- **Listen.** Putting staff or client suggestions into practice shows that you value their opinions and ideas. If it's a good idea, implement it and *give them the credit.*

Empower Growth

I want my employees to feel confident in both my support and their independence. I know how important it is to trust that my job will let me grow. The company I worked for immediately before starting TitleSmart didn't give me that confidence, and I knew I would never be able to stretch my legs and use my leadership skills.

I had a vision for creating a better customer experience. I knew that an enhanced customer experience was a clear, simple way to attract more clients, and I tried to communicate that to my leaders. All they said was, "Sure, do it for your own clients . . . nothing else is going to change." I knew that my contributions weren't reflected in my opportunities for growth, in responsibilities, pay, or title. So, I quit to start my own business.

Quitting was a big leap, and one that I'm grateful I was able to take. Not everyone is! But even if I hadn't quit, I was checked out. Employees who can't see a future do not give 100 percent. My old job could have taken advantage of my ideas, but instead they led me to be disillusioned with the company as a whole. All's well that ends well, because I'm thrilled to be running my own company how I want to ... and now, with growth for myself and my team in sight, I'm constantly giving 110 percent.

In order to establish my employees' long-term investment in TitleSmart, I work hard to communicate their options for growth within the company. I wouldn't expect a customer to wander around with no guidance— why would I expect my employees to do so?

I allow for career check-ins with my direct reports from time to time; they're looser than a review, but they ensure that we put aside time to talk about the future. I want my staff to have a clear structure for advancement, and to use it! I set annual and quarterly goals for myself and the company, and I ask my staff to set goals for themselves. By setting the example, I can challenge myself to dream big and expect the same of my team.

Tips by Cindy:

- **Be a mentor.** Get invested in your employees' futures so that they invest their future in your business.

- **Teach teachers.** You won't be able to mentor everyone around you, so pass that ability on to other high performers. Identify team members who can spread the company's mission and encourage a work ethic in others . . . and ask them to do so!

CHAPTER 6:
Positive Culture

I treat my employees like my favorite customers. Without my favorite customers, my business wouldn't be what it is ... and without my employees, it *really* wouldn't be what it is! Too many leaders focus on the numbers and forget that it's the people that make their business a success.

Finding ways to inject more positivity into your workplace will shift your business into a higher gear. Even if you're thinking, *"My company is already pretty happy and successful,"* consider what results you could produce if you and your team were even 10 percent happier!

I remember working at a company years ago that chose to stamp its return address on all its envelopes instead of just buying professional envelopes with the return address and logo. We *hated* stamping those addresses on! Not to mention the stamps weren't always straight (don't look at me). We asked to order branded envelopes and were turned down. This seems like a tiny story, but it was one of many at this company. As employees, we subconsciously interpreted those decisions to mean that the company wasn't willing to invest in professionalism or our happiness. And guess what? *I quit that job as soon as I could.*

The key to improved employee engagement and high retention is a positive culture. Don't underestimate the importance of happiness.

Tips by Cindy:

- **Give your employees what they need.** Don't be the office supply miser! I tell my staff that if they need anything from a certain type of pen to an updated computer program to do their job better, we will get it for them.

Accountability

Shit happens. Mistakes happen. **Step up and be honest about them**. Taking responsibility when you deserve it sets an example for everyone around you, whether or not you have authority over them. The best way to build trust with your boss, coworkers, team, or clients is to be accountable and take the hit when you do make a mistake. Don't bother trying to hide the truth ... employees can sense secrets like Sherlock Holmes, and they'll hunt for the truth like him, too!

Your boss will appreciate the honesty and see that you care about your job and performance. Your coworkers will appreciate that you didn't blame them for something that wasn't their fault. Your team and clients will appreciate and trust you for not jumping on the excuses train after a mistake.

Once you've leveled with your team, **be the change**. Advance your training and knowledge; the more eager you are to learn, the more people will want to teach you new things. **Learn from your mistakes.** Find a solution. At this point, the problem isn't going anywhere! Face it head-on and see where you end up. All my major learning has come from researching to solve a problem.

True trust is built when the people around you believe that you are taking steps to prevent the same slip-up in the future. Trust and loyalty are intimately connected, and they both are necessary for strong relationships. And remember: **businesses are built on relationships**.

Transparency

Employees want to feel included and invested in the direction of the business, especially at a small company. Be transparent about the state of the business and your hopes for it in the future!

Involve them in decision-making processes; even if you eventually don't act on their input, you acted to *receive* their input, creating a positive working culture. I like to invite our staff members to write for our company blog and staff newsletter. My only requirement is that they write about something upbeat or something that they are passionate about that will help or inspire.

Remember, honesty is the best policy no matter what circumstance you find yourself in.

Positive Team Playing

Teamwork is the driving force behind a successful business, small or large. There is no doubting this. A group's success has little to do with just one individual member—it depends more on how well the team works together. In 2016, we had a branch that completely fell apart due to a leader who was not contributing to the team or the business. Over time, this leader started doing less and less work and sharing less and less credit with her team members. The team members started feeling used and disgruntled, which resulted in the spreading of a cancer-like disease in our office. Ultimately, we said goodbye to the culprits who were only spreading negativity, and a handful of staff from another branch jumped in with me and worked long hours to rebuild the office. I'm grateful to have team members who can replace pessimism with optimism, because **individual attitudes affect the whole business.**

It's not uncommon to find yourself on a team with a negative atmosphere or poor performance—and more often than not, these two traits are connected. Successful teams have strong, progress-oriented dynamics and can manage healthy conflict. In other words, they kick ass!

We've all been there: you had an uncomfortable conversation with someone at work and now it feels like there's a thick cloud of tension hanging over the office. It's normal to want to shrug tough conversations off and pretend like they never happened, but that can actually do more harm than good. By ignoring the conversation that took place you're also giving up your chance to make some important changes that could benefit both of you in the long run.

Whether you're butting heads over a project or over something much bigger, it's important to follow up to make sure there's a plan in place to resolve the issue at hand.

So, what can you do to make things less awkward and move forward?

- **Acknowledge that the conversation happened.** Instead of avoiding your colleague, make it a point to acknowledge that the conversation took place. Proactively follow up by expressing that you appreciate being able to come together to identify and discuss issues when they arise. It's okay to admit that it was a tough situation, but be sure to focus on the positive. Thank your colleague for taking the time to work through this with you.

- **Move the conversation forward.** Take action to resolve the issue at hand by brainstorming ways you and your colleague can move forward. Even if you were only able to agree on a few points during your conversation, use areas of common ground to come up with a plan that works for both of you.

- **Focus on building a relationship with your colleague.** At the end of the day you and your colleague are both human. Keep in mind that deep down, every human being wants to be liked—especially at work. If the only interaction you have with each other is when a difficult situation arises, they might start avoiding you or associating you with uncomfortable meetings. Focus on the bigger picture and think about what kind of work relationship you want to have with your colleagues.

Start small by learning more about their goals and who they are as a person through casual conversation. Invite them to get coffee with you during your lunch break or make it a point to share time together at your next off-site work event. Making friends and building relationships takes a little work. Remember, it's just a little work.

The Art of No Sinkholes

If you are on or manage a team that doesn't ever seem to move forward, work to identify the **sinkholes**—issues that have the potential to collapse out from under you and your team. First, decide if *you* are the sinkhole (or problem). Even if you never admit it to anyone else, *work to admit it to yourself . . .* and then work to change your behavior, influence the group, and steer the team to success!

- **Address issues immediately.** I find that if someone snaps at you or offends you in some way, it's best to ask them politely and professionally why they said that or simply let them know how their actions make you feel. The key here is to be polite and professional and address the situation immediately when it happens. This communicates your boundaries right away and gives the other person the responsibility to do the work by fixing the situation or responding to you. When confronted with this technique, typically people respond right away with, "Oh, I'm sorry, I didn't realize

I came across that way," or, "I didn't mean to snap back that way." Situation immediately defused. Practice and learn this skill and don't let things fester. No need to go crying to the HR department or upper management to fight your battles for you. This is an adult skill.

- **Never stop learning.** New approaches to solving old problems can revitalize an entire team. When a challenge comes up, dig in deeper to the topic at hand instead of passing the buck to someone else. One of my signature statements is to take responsibility for your learning—don't wait around for people to show you something, teach yourself, and ask a lot of questions.

- **Up your enthusiasm.** A project that seems doomed drags down your energy, which only dooms the project even more, easily slipping into a cycle. Tell yourself to walk into the next meeting with energy for the issue and your coworkers! I know this is easier said than done, but this is what I do: I throw some "Rocky punches" in the air, dance around a little bit with my arms up, and make sure to keep my eyebrows up (with your eyebrows up, it is impossible to be or sound cranky). Trust me—sometimes I don't feel like doing it, but it's just mind over matter. Suck it up and just do it!

- **React professionally.** This is work, not a soap opera. Focus on issues, not on individuals. If you have a hard time separating a person from a problem, take yourself out of the situation physically or mentally (or both). Walk a lap around the office, count to ten, breathe, and consider an outsider's perspective on the issue.

The more you know, the more you can do. The more you can do, the more opportunities exist for you. The more opportunities exist for you, the more you can climb in your career.

CHAPTER 7:
Show Appreciation

Remember in the last chapter when I said, "Treat your employees like your favorite customer?" This chapter, I'm asking you to go one step further and *recognize* their work and accomplishments.

When your staff feel valued, they in turn value their work and the company. Every action that your employees take has the potential to help the business—so motivate them to make small, positive impacts every day by demonstrating appreciation for their efforts. Your team members are financially invested in the company and its outcome, and they should be emotionally invested, too . . . but it's hard to pour emotional investment into a workplace if they don't feel like the workplace is emotionally invested in them! That's where your appreciation and recognition come in.

Tips by Cindy:

- **Pay attention to the small stuff.** Keep track of employees' birthdays, small successes, and personal or professional milestones. And then, *acknowledge them.*

Show Appreciation for Their Effort

Your staff put more waking hours into your business than they do into any other part of their lives. Show gratitude for their effort by respecting their input and time! Treat the staff member like they are your best customer!

Listen to Their Ideas

Let your staff know that their ideas are important. If my staff gives me a suggestion that I like, I get excited and build on that energy to implement it as soon as possible. Plus, hearing ideas for improvements from my staff takes some of the work off my plate!

Great ideas are more likely to be implemented if they come with a clear pathway to success. If you are suggesting a change, do the work upfront before presenting it. And if your team is batting around ideal scenarios, ask them to work out how exactly to get there.

The tricky part is when I don't like their idea. In the spirit of transparency, I try to be as honest as possible, and oftentimes I like and want to use bits and pieces of their ideas. Then, together we can brainstorm to an entirely new idea or concept. I always make sure I am upfront with others and ask them to be the same with my ideas. Recently, I let my creative team know that I wanted to start polling on my website and social media platforms. Honestly, we have changed our ideas and formats on this at least ten times and it is still evolving and expanding. Everything from the tech platform to the poll questions have been interactive with my team and me. Even many of my ideas have been shot down by the team and revamped. It's a true collaborative process.

Make Work Comfortable

There's a reason that wildly successful tech start-ups have beer fridges, ping-pong tables, and free food: **when a workplace makes employees' lives easier and happier, they are more dedicated to the actual work.**

Making their workdays easier means they will work harder for you. You don't have to go as far as Whiskey Wednesday Afternoons, but there are many concrete steps you can take in making the workplace inviting.

The simplest solution is food and drinks. If you don't offer coffee, spring for it, and watch your employees' eyes bug out. If you do provide coffee, spring for the nicer stuff! Or add snacks: fruit and granola bars are easy to pick up and encourage healthy breaks. Each TitleSmart office receives a delivery of healthy breakfast, lunch, and snack items every week. We want to make sure our employees have easy access to  nutritious food throughout the day while they're at work. We weren't always able to do this. Early on we picked up items from Costco or Sam's Club on sale and even brought things from home to share.

At TitleSmart, our PTO program combines paid sick days and vacation days into one bank that employees can use however they choose. We allow employees to roll over their PTO each year, and we also give them the option to "cash out" and get paid for up to 40 hours of PTO if they choose.

After five years of service, we offer a "sabbatical." Our employees receive an additional 15 days of paid vacation plus $5,000 in travel expenses as my way of saying thank you and ensuring that they can explore the world outside work. We couldn't always offer this special incentive, but as we rounded the decade toward our ten-year anniversary, the business had grown enough for me to be looking for unique ways to reward staff and increase retention. I was inspired by a much larger business, and I set the travel allowance and "sabbatical" length to appropriate levels for our budget and staff.

I fully realize that not every company can offer these types of benefits—and frankly, not all of them would appeal to employees across all industries. Get creative with affordable perks and benefits. Is it a wellness room? A paid cab ride home from the company party?

Ask your employees what would matter most to them. Getting feedback:

- Makes them feel heard

- Makes them feel appreciated

- Makes them love their job

Plus, when they are personally invested in their benefits, they are less poachable by your competitors.

Tips by Cindy:

- **Birthday PTO.** I believe that birthdays should stay special throughout adulthood! I added Birthday PTO to our benefits package because I think everyone should be able to take a day off work to enjoy their birthday. If a birthday lands on a holiday or a weekend, then the employee can use it whenever they would like.

Make Work Fun

Work shouldn't be all pressure and grind! Schedule birthday breakfasts, baby showers over the lunch hour, and holiday gift exchanges. Embracing celebration and fun at work gives employees a much-needed break and builds relationships.

At TitleSmart, I obsess about our holiday party. I want the holiday season to feel special and generous, so I work with my staff to plan a killer party! When the team was small, I took the few of us out to dinner, but now with a much larger staff the sky is the limit. In the past few years, we hosted a "casino night" with drinks and raffles and threw a Roaring 20's themed party with a live band. Of course, you don't have to go all-out. I happen to love throwing parties—but if you love smaller gatherings, or seeing a show, then have people over to your house, or reserve a block of tickets to a touring Broadway musical. Whatever you do, make it fun!

Show Recognition

We all want to be recognized. Whether you dream of being complimented privately or celebrated with a plaque on the wall, each one of us craves positive affirmation in some form. And that includes your employees! They want to know that the work they are doing is making a difference. At our holiday party, we have a full ceremony with awards.

Consider these strategies for visibly recognizing successes:

- **Shout-outs in emails or on social media.**
  From time to time, send a note to your team calling out one person's work from that week. I like doing this randomly with no method to my madness so it's always a fun surprise! As an employee, you should take responsibility for getting noticed. Our staff are competitive and tell each other, "Game On!" This may not work in every office environment, so go with your

gut, test the waters, and customize to see what works for you.

- **Miscellaneous milestones and achievements**. At TitleSmart, we like to celebrate all the little things, from a milestone anniversary to a bridal shower. Whether I bring it up at lunch or call it out in the quarterly staff newsletter, it's the little things that make the big difference.

- **Add it to your one-on-one agenda.** Think of a recent success, and *write it down*!

It's too often that leaders forget to simply say, "Hey, I really appreciate all of your hard work recently. It means a lot to me and the company as a whole." You can give people benefits until you're blue in the face, but sometimes your employees just need to hear that they and their work are important.

Financial Recognition

You've probably been wondering, "When is she going to talk about the cash?!" There's a reason I put it last: monetary rewards carry the most weight, but there can be so many non-monetary benefits with a huge value proposition.

That said, I won't deny that **money talks**. When there is a financial carrot at the end of the stick, employees want to contribute to the growth and success of the business. They have a vested interest in making an impact, which in turn leads them to work harder and smarter for you.

I have given holiday bonuses to my staff based on service and contribution to the company *every year except our first year in business*. If TitleSmart made a profit, even a small one, I have always wanted to share it with the staff who made it possible.

I also love to give random, unexpected spot bonuses. If we were extra busy and one of my employees busted their butt, it just blows them away to find an extra $500 in their paycheck without mention. Someone worked hard, and I noticed it—I want my employees to know I'm paying attention.

Give raises and bonus incentives to staff when they are deserved—never before they are deserved, but also never after. If your company is having a great year, or your staff is giving 100 percent, let them know they deserve a slice of the pie they made. Pay attention to when raises are warranted . . . *and give them before staff have to come asking for them.* If you can afford it, give spot bonuses—they can be very powerful to encourage loyalty and reward great work. Strive to pay top wages and include an incentive plan—**if another company can't afford your employees, they become un-poachable!** You can also provide other fun perks like staff apparel or sporting event tickets. Recently I bought myself a really great cashmere wrap while traveling. I knew my team was working hard to hold down the fort while I was gone, so when I came back, I ordered them all wraps too!

Part III:
Your Customers

CHAPTER 8:
Your Royal Court

Presentation of the Establishment

Service builds relationships, relationships build business. I cannot make it clear enough. Your customers' decisions are influenced by service whether they are conscious of it or not, so don't let service be where you fall down. With that said, service together with an outstanding presentation makes a lasting first impression.

The Customer Is King

I've heard "the customer is always right" about a billion times. It's what was drilled into my head from the time I was 14 and working at a drug store checkout onward. *The customer is always right.* I choose to take this one step further: **The customer is king.**

Piss off the king, and you'll regret it! If you fall from favor, it could be *off with your head!* Even when a customer is getting under your skin, it's never worth proving a point. Which will you prioritize: getting even in the moment, or your business/career for years into the future?

Make the king happy, and you shall be rewarded and rise! Meet your customers' needs—and anticipate those needs before they do. Remember who your business serves!

Tips by Cindy:

- **Ask for feedback.** Whether it's an anonymous survey after a deal with your client or an in-person meeting, solicit your customers' perspectives. It's the fastest way to improve.

Customer-Centric Decisions

I expect almost every conversation that takes place on TitleSmart time to at least *mention* our customers. Every choice is made with our customers in mind, from big decisions like who we hire and how we structure our teams to day-to-day details like how we answer the phone and how we decorate our conference rooms.

Maybe this seems obvious! But think about your company: are any decisions driven strictly by costs? Employee tension or complaints? Too frequently, the customer is an afterthought. But to realize true success, you must obsess about the customer experience.

I love doing closings for first time homebuyers. Since the process is stressful and intimidating, oftentimes they are terrified by the time they get to the closing table. Sometimes they are actually shaking. This is when I take a moment to touch their arm and tell them to just be in the moment. I explain to them that there are a lot of moving parts and stimulation and tell them to just focus their attention on me. This helps to calm them and better enable them to enjoy the process. This is their first house—it's a big deal!

Quote Your Customer

Ask for customer feedback, and *listen to it*. Share it with your leaders, peers, and team. This applies to both negative *and* positive feedback: any customer perspective is gold. Knowing your customers' perspective will keep their voices in your head at all times.

You will get negative feedback; every business does. Don't dilute it! Watering down or dismissing remarks only removes your own accountability. "They're crazy for thinking that! And it's for sure not our fault . . ." Address the concern as quickly as possible—it's on you to continually better your business.

Share positive testimonials, too. Positive feedback reinforces great business behavior and makes your team feel validated for their hard work. Plus, it keeps the customer in focus for employees who don't interact directly with clients. At TitleSmart, we send a quick, short survey to recent customers asking for feedback . . . both positive and negative. I share the responses with my staff, study long-term trends, and post positive snippets on our website and social media. I aim to get as much mileage out of every positive comment as humanly possible, internally and externally! Naturally, this also gives me the opportunity to make a wrong right with a negative review and make the customer feel that their feedback really *does* matter.

Make Your Office Friendly

Your office should be a place that customers want to come to. Nothing turns a consumer off from a business like disliking the experience of actually being there! I put a ton of energy into making TitleSmart locations welcoming and high-energy. So much so, that our customers end up stopping by when they are in the area! I tell them that they can always swing in to grab hot cocoa or a cookie. We will always make time for them, and the office will always be upbeat and fun.

Greet Them with a Smile

The minute your customers walk into your office, their first impression affects their entire experience. They are your livelihood, so establish a comfortable rapport right away! Infuse your space with positivity and personalization with a few of these ideas:

- Have someone at the front desk to greet your customers with a pleasant and energetic welcome.

- Attend to each customer immediately; don't leave people waiting. I have seriously walked out on appointments when I've been left unacknowledged for long periods of time and never returned.

- Offer them amenities like beverages (more on that later).

- Check in regularly if they will be waiting for a bit. Or, just don't keep them waiting!

Nowadays, many companies have nearly eliminated reception areas—especially in the real estate industry, it's normal to not have anyone at the front desk. But I believe the best thing for my customers is a friendly greeting from a real person, whether on the phone or at the front desk. To truly personalize an experience, it has to be personal from the get-go.

Tips by Cindy:

- **Bring the happy.** Be the bearer of happiness when you are out and about. One of TitleSmart's signatures is having fresh cookies baking in the office throughout the day, and when I go to another company or location for a closing, I bring a little bag of fresh-baked cookies to share. No one will ever forget me or my company!

Décor Matters

Making your office a pleasant place is essential to the customer experience. Warm colors and modern furnishings immediately communicate to your clients that you care about them. I am out at other title companies for closings all the time, and I'm flabbergasted at how outdated and dumpy some of them are. Unpleasant décor sends the message that a company doesn't care about its image, which never reflects well on how much it cares about its work.

Tips by Cindy:

- **Refresh your decor.** Every few years, ask your employees to point out décor that should be updated . . . and make the change! And remember, keep things pristine and neat.

- **Decorate for holidays.** Neutral holiday decorations spread charm and personality, and make a space feel cozier and more welcoming.

Provide Amenities

I was out at a closing the other day at one of the biggest title companies in the Twin Cities, and on their table was a sign that said, "For the courtesy of others, please turn off your cell phone." I had to stop myself from yelling, *"What?!"* Of all the things you could choose to put on your table, why would you choose that? Instead of "Have an exciting closing!" or "Have a great day," they chose to inconvenience their customers. In our offices we say, "Hey! Here's our wi-fi login—go set up shop." I want our customers to be as comfortable as possible and to have the option of being productive while waiting. Time is a valuable commodity.

Think of ways to stand out in customer comfort. Some ideas include:

- **Beverages:** Water, soda, hot cocoa, tea, and **good** coffee (not brown water) all make an impact.

- **Food:** Go above and beyond with hot cookies or cold snacks.

- **Current Reading:** There's nothing worse than being in an office that only has magazines from a year ago, or publications that no one wants to read. I don't care that I'm at the dentist, I don't want to read *Oral Health Magazine*!

- **Wi-fi:** Your customers might be waiting, so encourage them to get work done and make themselves at home. Don't skimp on wi-fi!

Offer Trinkets

Before you laugh off branded knick-knacks, consider this story. Years ago, I was managing another title company and I had ordered trendy clear pens to give out like crazy to my customers, vendors, and friends. About a year later, I was shopping at Sam's Club and the cashier handed me a pen to sign my credit card receipt . . . and it was the pen from my company. I thought to myself right away, "Mission accomplished!" How many people knew the name of my company from that pen's travels?!

Tips by Cindy:

- **Spread out the trinkets.** Branded trinkets should be available in the lobby and meeting spaces—no one needs to miss out! And don't get stale with the trinkets you offer . . . make sure you are changing these out from year to year.

Some unique branded trinket ideas:

- Reading glasses (this is our most popular item!)

- Pop sockets and phone gadgets

- USB car chargers and tech items

- Candies (our customers love sea salt caramels!)

- Lip balms and lotions (name brand, of course!)

- Kitchen utensils (duh, new home!)

- Notepads (see "Art of the Checkbox" in chapter 2)

- Apparel (everyone loves our extra-thin hoodie!)

In the service industry, if you compete on service and amenities, then you don't need to compete on price. The competition can always undercut your prices, but their reputation will spin customers away from them, into your doors.

CHAPTER 9:
Always Be Present

Constant presence is critical as you build a business. Be a part of your customers' lives, even on the outskirts, and they will be a part of yours.

I want my name to be the first name people think of when they think of title and home closing. That's my mantra. I want to be a constant presence in the real estate world, both for real estate partners and customers. If I am always present in title thoughts and conversations, my business will grow from sheer math!

Strong relationships help make you the go-to in your industry for your network (and their network). So keep following those rules: show appreciation, invest in the customer experience even after a project or sale, and get personal.

Last year, we changed radio partners and began advertising on a new station. The difference was immediately astounding: our new sales representative and her manager extend regular notes and reminders to me that make me want to continue our relationship. It's not like our previous partner was bad; they just didn't understand the concept of always being present. And you bet I plan to stay with this radio representative for the foreseeable future!

Tips by Cindy:

- **Don't let connections wither on the vine.** Stay in touch after a project or sale, and foster connections long after they seem to be completed.

Online Presence

When I first opened TitleSmart in 2007, I made our website an immediate necessity. Not even a priority: a *necessity*. Businesses were using the internet at that time, of course, but it wasn't unheard of for small companies to forgo an online presence because it seemed too expensive, foreign, or unimportant. But I insisted we be present in every facet, so I hired a college student to make a cheap, clean site.

Two years later, I worked with a mid-level web designer to revamp the site ... and after our ten-year anniversary I revamped our site yet again! I still look at it several times each week wondering what I can do to stay ahead of my competition. I don't like to become complacent with anything in my business, especially not our web presence. When someone wants to find out about TitleSmart, they're going to Google us!

Website

Site design doesn't have to be intimidating—think of it in drafts. You can always (and *should* always) go back and update content and structure, but you've gotta get something on the board. If you're unsatisfied with your website, block off time to improve it ... *now.* Keep content current. I crack right up when I know an employee left a company and I still see them on their website months later—lazy!

Make a better site than your competitors. I am often told by my competition that our website is fantastic and they spy on it regularly. If you don't have an eye or a budget for online improvements, check out similar businesses in other areas of the country for fresh ideas. And when you can afford it, hire a site designer to consult on how to make yours stand out. Make sure your site:

- Is easy to navigate

- Has a unique look

- Reflects the company's brand and personality

- Offers handy tools to introduce and preview your services

- Displays all accreditations, associations, and achievements

- Features staff and customer testimonials

A great site adds credibility to your business and opens new relationships.

Social Media

If you've already bought into social media, great! If it's not your thing . . . too bad! It's the way of the world now, and your customers are on social media platforms. The best part about social media is that it is free (at least until you pay a professional social media company to do the research, data prep, and posting for you). At TitleSmart, I managed our company Facebook, LinkedIn, and Twitter for the first few years. In 2014, I finally set a budget and started working with a social media firm, and it's been worth every penny. No matter how you manage your presence on social media, you have to do it, and do it well. Adding the professional social media element to our marketing efforts was a game changer for my business, and now we are leading the industry and are an example for others in our market.

Here are a few tips to get started:

- **Start small.** Create a company Facebook page and start posting. You should have seen my first company Facebook page! It was comical, but I was learning and I like to learn by doing.

- **Do you know a millennial?** They are great at social media! Talk one of them into helping you create a page and teaching you a few tricks.

- **Google.** There are tons of how-to instructions for the layman on Google.

- **Add new platforms.** Once you get comfortable with Facebook, consider adding Instagram, Twitter, Pinterest, or any platform where your customers are lurking.

Sometimes a closer will ask me, "How can I increase my business?" My answer is always the same, and it's a question. "How much are you doing on social media?" They say, "Oh, that's right . . ." Then they scoot back to their computers and start working!

Once you have a lot of followers or likes on your newly created Facebook (for *us*, 1,000 followers was a lot!), consider running advertisements, which can increase traffic to your website, improve search rankings, and narrow down the group of people you're trying to reach. My goal is to reach realtors, lenders, and people who are buying or selling a home, and ads help me get in front of those people.

But it's not just about advertising. Your presence on social media helps you connect with your customers, learn more about them personally and as a demographic, and *always be present* in the back of their minds.

Tips by Cindy:

- **Get an expert to run your social media.**
  If you don't feel like an aficionado, then hire a staff member or contract with a firm who specializes in social media strategy. Worth it!

- **Get an expert to create your website.**
  Exactly the same as above . . . worth it!

Keep up with the Work and Do It Quickly

Once you've established consistency in the market, you've got to follow through. Demonstrate that you are not only willing to go above and beyond, but you are capable as well.

Don't expect to slide by understaffed. Your clients will go elsewhere if you are behind and don't have the appropriate support. If you need to hire more people, do it! The upfront cost will be outweighed by customer satisfaction and continued business. Having adequate staff enables you to handle the case load and work ahead.

Quick turnaround shows your customers that you respect their time. Communicate your passion and dedication through actions, not only words. The proof will be in the pudding.

This applies to communication, too. I get so much referral business just because I respond faster than my competition. Slow response time sends a message to a customer that their email wasn't even important enough to merit a quick note. I covered this in chapter 2, but it bears repeating: if you are unreachable, chances are your competitor is around and ready to answer a call from your customer.

Be a constant presence for your customers throughout their whole interaction with your industry. If they are at another stage in the process, getting support from you (even when you're not obligated to be involved) will only cement their loyalty. Viewing our customers' overall experience has led us to find new and better ways to proactively communicate the critical role we play.

Even if one of our real estate partners is handling part of a transaction without me or my team, we always make ourselves available as sounding boards. We appreciate their business, and I want TitleSmart to be associated with all things real estate!

Tips by Cindy:

- **Be present in communications**. It's all about response time—stay at the top of your customers' minds!

Get Creative

One of my main strategies for being constantly present in my network is my branded trinkets ... but we've talked enough about those! Figure out how you might be able to spread the word about your team's expertise. Consider a few ideas:

- **Personal (mailed to their home) mailings.** These can be business-related or just notes to remind people they matter to you and your company.

- **Newsletters.** Keep your network up to date on your great work and industry news.

- **Accreditation.** TitleSmart is woman-owned, so we are members of organizations that support women in business. Consider what professional associations might be a good fit for your company—it's great networking, and often free advertising.

- **Press.** A year after starting TitleSmart, I contacted the local newspaper about a feature story. Sure enough, they ran an article about our budding business—and two years later, they revisited our company to tell our amazing growth story. A couple of years later, TitleSmart was featured in the *Minnesota Business Journal,* and all three articles created buzz in the community and our industry.

- **Awards.** Seek nominations for awards that are appropriate for your business. The free advertising and recognition can last for years. We research awards we would like to qualify for, then we ask someone to nominate us. It is as simple as that. Remember, friends help friends.

- **Press releases.** Anything new going on about your business is possible news. Moving your offices or a company milestone are great excuses to put something out on the wire for media publications to pick up and spread the good word. The first time somebody told me I needed to do a press release, I was like "How do you do that?" So I started asking around and did some online searching and found a good website to just walk me through the process. There are a lot of good ones out there, but I like PRWeb.com. It's like setting up your online banking, it will walk you through the prompts, and once you get one under your belt, you will be a pro!

Tips by Cindy:

- **Stretch your marketing.** Consider every avenue for getting the word out, and follow through. When you have a great narrative, use it, use it, and use it again!

CHAPTER 10:
Set Yourself Apart

It's pretty straightforward to create a good customer experience: follow the tips from the last two chapters. But to create an *outstanding* customer experience, you have to think differently from the market. You have to go above and beyond, stretching yourself and your company to stand above the competition.

You have to obsess about the customer experience. It's all I think about. What more can we do to create an outstanding experience for our customer? I love taking little ideas and running with them. A year after founding TitleSmart, I joked with a customer, "We should take a red carpet picture to celebrate!" That image stuck

in my head, and a few years later I ordered a company logo backdrop and an actual red carpet so we can photograph first time homebuyers celebrating their new home purchase with a bottle of branded, celebratory champagne. Every step in the customer experience can always be improved when you obsess to success.

Not too long ago, I was working with a husband and wife who were in the process of getting a divorce. This situation was a little tricky as there was a restraining order in place. I knew early on that extra care would be needed on my part. The morning of the closing, one of the parties decided at the last minute to attend the closing instead of signing early—this threw a wrench into the restraining order situation. I immediately called the other party, and was able to run out and meet with them to quickly sign papers and avoid a head-on collision. The experience as well as the safety of my client was at the forefront of every step of that process. Additionally, both clients sent me follow up thank-you notes for personally walking them through this difficult and emotional process.

Identify Pain Points

Every industry is flush with experiences that are frustrating for consumers. In the title industry, customers are most frequently disappointed when closings are delayed or don't go smoothly . . . which happens *all the time*. TitleSmart tackles that common pain point by hiring the most experienced closers in the industry and doing detailed legwork upfront to ensure we've identified and dealt with any red flags well in advance of the closing.

Consider your own industry's pain points. What would you complain about if you were a customer in your industry? What are the most common "horror stories"? Rather than dismissing these as unavoidable, get creative about how you can step ahead of your competitors and make life easier for your customers.

Solve the Little Problems, Too

After the big pain points are addressed, brainstorm secondary concerns and help your customers feel confident walking through your industry. I know that my customers are often unsure of what to expect on the day of closing, so TitleSmart sends a warm, welcoming email that includes a photo of their closer and outlines the process. Supporting your customers through every step of the process sets you apart from the rest of the market.

Watch for your customers' needs and address them. Recently, I was working with a realtor partner whose phone died—and a realtor with a dead phone is like a plumber with no tools. Instead of being annoyed at him, I started brainstorming: what if we provided a charging station in every branch? We now provide a multi-phone charging station in every office, and it's been a huge hit. Go above and beyond, and your customers will notice!

Tips by Cindy:

- **Put yourself in their shoes.** What would bug you about your own industry if you were in the customers' shoes? What would make you feel special? Make decisions with those perspectives in mind!

Create Memorable Moments

Successful businesses are magnetic because of their unique personalities—and their ability to communicate those personalities through memorable moments. Embrace your own quirks or those of your business to create signature "moves."

You already know how much I love branded trinkets (I leaned into that love early in running my company)! Trinkets are now a TitleSmart hallmark, and my customers love them because they are my way of clearly communicating my personality. Frankly, it doesn't matter if someone else thinks they're cheesy; authentic cheesiness is way more magnetic than faux "coolness."

I also love the holiday season, so I go all-out with our holiday card. I treat it as another opportunity to connect with my customers and thank them for a great year of business. My team writes clever industry-specific parodies of holiday songs to make it stand out, and our phones always start ringing a couple days later after we mail them, with customers loving the parody lyrics.

Both of these are totally reflective of my personal taste and my vision for the company, and I don't expect you to love holiday greeting cards as much as I do. But I *do* expect you to dig into what makes you magnetic and let that honesty spread throughout all of your work. I frequently joke around with my customers by covering my name badge and saying, "What's my name?!" They're often sheepish about having forgotten it, but I make it a game—and by the next time I make the same joke, I assure you that they remember my name. Find your own playfulness and pump it into your entire business.

Tips by Cindy:

- **Remember the little things.** Did you find out that your customer loves sailing? When you write their thank-you note, do it on a card with a sailboat. Make it clear that you were paying close attention.

Be the First

Four years ago, I met a vendor at an industry conference with a prototyped title app, and I immediately said, **"I have to have it."** He didn't think I was serious ... but you better believe that within thirty days, I had contracted with that vendor and launched our own version.  We were the first company in Minnesota to launch this offering to customers, and it's now the industry-leading title app that provides customers with fee quotes. Our competition is still in the dust—even with similar products, the TitleSmart name is associated with convenience and innovation.

It is absolutely critical that you seize innovation when you see it. Set yourself apart from your competition and be ready to embrace change rather than resist it. When I attend title industry events, I make it my top priority to visit vendor tables and look for the latest technology and trends—and I contact the vendors immediately. Occasionally, the vendors are slow to respond, almost as if they are surprised to hear such enthusiasm and a desire for such quick implementation; that was the vendor's reaction when I asked for our fee quote app to be launched ASAP! But speed is the key separator between you and your competition. Eventually everyone will use the new technology (or fold altogether), so it's in your best interest to be the first.

At TitleSmart, everything we do is about being the first and the best—setting ourselves apart.

Tips by Cindy:

- **Fill the gaps.** Identify what your competitors are missing and deliver. Word will spread. For my company and industry, I noticed that everyone seemed to be competing on price rather than the overall customer experience. Too many companies place a high level of emphasis on being the lowest price in the market, and I really think they are missing the ball here. Many times price isn't the deciding factor in a customer's decision to come back or, more importantly, refer friends and family your way to help build your business. This is exactly why I talk about the customer experience all the time. A great customer experience is what builds brand loyalty and brings people back. Try to pinpoint what you are doing better than your competitors or where you can fill the gap to drive customers to your business.

Empathy and Accountability

There's a moment we all dread: something went wrong and you have an angry customer on your hands. Even one unhappy customer can spell disaster for a company's reputation—but tense and uncomfortable moments can also present opportunities. Handling an upset customer with care and concern not only resolves the current issue but can lead to a stronger long-term relationship.

Stepping up and taking responsibility for your actions builds trust in a relationship with a customer—just like with your employees (see chapter 6). Failing to address an issue only lets negative emotions fester and rot; that could result in your business's reputation taking a hit. When one of my staff members is facing an upset customer, I tell them my five steps:

1. **Apologize quickly.** It's not always the most pleasant item on your to-do-list, but taking care of an unhappy customer has to be a top priority. The longer the person is left feeling frustrated or angry, the worse the situation becomes—so rearrange your day to address it if needed. The first thing out of your mouth, whether it's your fault or not, should be, "I'm sorry."

2. **Stay calm.** It's easy to panic when something goes wrong. Instead of imagining the worst-case scenario or dwelling on what caused the problem in the first place, determine a logical plan to solve the problem. I like to call it the Art of Distraction. When I'm working on a solution, I don't have time to panic.

3. **Practice empathy.** It's uncomfortable to imagine how the customer felt or thought as

a result of a mistake. But instead of shying away from that feeling, it pays to dig and really think through what you would want to hear and experience if it happened to you. Demonstrating empathy communicates that you understand their frustration or anger and that you are taking the incident seriously— which in turn helps make the customer more receptive to a solution.

4. **Propose a solution and deliver.** Take an immediate action to resolve the problem, and lay out a timeline if more steps are needed. Do everything you can to make the person feel especially cared for and important; now is the most important time to go above and beyond to make things happen quickly and efficiently for the customer.

5. **Say thank you.** Let the customer know you appreciate the fact that they brought the issue to your attention and were willing to stick with you as you resolved it. This small gesture demonstrates a commitment to improvement

and invites the customer to be part of making things better, now and in the future.

These steps have helped me and my team stay positive and focused, even when things don't go exactly as planned. Every interaction with a customer is an opportunity to go beyond their expectations, so don't run from your upset customers—embrace them.

CHAPTER 11:
Everyone Eats

You know your company wouldn't run without you, your team, or your customers. But there is one more big chunk of people who keep your business chugging along . . . *your vendors*. How would your employees run their reports if their software systems were crashing? What would your customers think of your dedication to service if your building were falling apart? You might keep your ship sailing straight ahead, but vendors keep it afloat.

Keep Your Vendors Happy

It's in your best interest to have happy vendor partners. Maybe it's easy to ignore their emails or bump their requests down your priority list without any immediate repercussions, but someday you'll need them, *pronto*. Those are the times when it pays to treat vendors well.

Treating your vendors well means your business gets their best work. Where do you think you currently are on your vendors' priority lists? Are you happy with that? Now consider how your team interacts with them—the patterns are likely related. A few years ago, we needed a new server . . . and fast. I asked our computer guys if it was possible to install the server over the weekend to avoid disrupting our work during the week. This vendor normally doesn't offer weekend service, but I always go above and beyond for them by referring them to others and always pay our bills promptly—that's a big one! Naturally, they made an exception for us, and I will be forever grateful. Some of their staff even crash our annual holiday party because we have such a great working relationship, and I love it!

Tips by Cindy:

- **Give recognition.** Does this sound familiar? It should! Strong relationships build good businesses, and recognition is one of the foundations of strong relationships. Think about how you would congratulate a customer on their success or thank an employee for going out of their way to be a good partner—*do that with your vendors!*

Celebrate with Everyone

Celebrate with everyone! The people and companies who helped you and your business achieve success should share in the "luv." Invite your vendor partners to

company gatherings, give them customer-level treatment, and treat them like staff.

Think back to the reciprocal relationship I mentioned above. Remember, positivity is

contagious; strong relationships only strengthen other relationships. If you've treated your vendors with respect and enthusiasm, they'll be there on the day you need them to come through. **When they eat, you eat.**

Everyone Is a Customer, Even Vendors

Don't forget that your vendors can also become your customers! It's very typical for our vendors to use us for their closings, because they understand how much we care about our customers. It's natural that when they have the opportunity, they become a customer too, making it more critical that we make them feel important. At TitleSmart, we make a concentrated effort to include our vendors on our invite lists for corporate events and new office grand openings.

Plus, introducing your vendor partners to your clients and customers gives your vendors opportunities to network. This won't lead your vendor away from you—in fact, giving them the gift of networking will only cement their loyalty to you. I close most personal transactions for my vendors, because they have become my clients. They trust TitleSmart to be sharp, fast, and detailed in title and closings, because that's how we treat them every day.

Tips by Cindy:

- **Refer new business.** You know how important it is to get positive referrals about your own business; give that gift to your partners, too.

Smart Referrals

Vendors don't exist on an island. They are business people just like you, so they are looking to grow their company. And they are consumers just like your clients—so they could ultimately be clients, too!

You add value to your relationship with a vendor by making connections easier for them. Vouching for a company and giving the gift of new business is a source of grounded power in a relationship. You wouldn't toss around names willy-nilly, and you wouldn't ask for new connections from just any old Joe Schmo—the referral of business is the highest compliment you can give.

I've started getting some of my suits custom-made by a professional clothier over the past couple years, and recently my tailor told me that he was planning to buy a house. I asked him if he had chosen a realtor, and he sheepishly explained that he was working with a friend's mom as his realtor. I rolled my eyes and said, "Does your friend's mom buy suits from you?" He immediately understood my point. Later he thanked me for teaching him the importance of intentionally making choices to enhance and grow his business.

Tips by Cindy:

- **Pay attention.** The people around you are expressing their needs all the time without meaning to. If my friend complains about the poor customer service at a business, I immediately tell them about *my* contact and *the experience* I had. When an acquaintance mentions that a family member is getting married, I immediately mention that when they are ready for a realtor, I can make strong recommen- dations—and, duh, that they should use TitleSmart!

Set the Example

It's on you to tip the first domino—you will set a trend that they can follow! They might mirror your behavior immediately, or they might be focused on the new energy of a potential customer, but either way, you will reap the rewards of their own referrals in the future. **Friends help friends and referrals build loyalty and trust.**

Tips by Cindy:

- **Be passionate.** The easiest sells come when you are passionate about the products or people—you instantly tell a more dynamic story. Find a way to get passionate about the referrals you're making . . . and refer people and businesses you're passionate about!

Referrals Aren't Always Intentional

The most powerful perspectives are those given in total honesty, when we aren't *trying* to vouch for anyone. Pay attention to how you talk about other business-people and companies, and how your friends, family, and partners talk about their recent experiences. People are always communicating their needs and wants, even if they don't realize it!

The way you talk about a company is a referral in and of itself. Dropping a compliment about a vendor partner, without making it a formal recommendation, goes a long way toward improving that company's reputation. I love my nail salon, and after going there for years, I care about the owner and her business. Sometimes I invite friends to join me for a manicure and introduce them to the owner . . . and funny enough, I run into those same friends when I go back! I love knowing that I'm supporting a small business run by a woman who I care about.

This principle applies to your vendors. When a person or company likes working with you, they will talk about you with their friends, family, and industry partners. This is the exact kind of unintentional referral that will bring new customers and other excellent vendors to your doorstep. But remember: the principle applies in the inverse, too. If you piss someone off, you better believe that word will get around . . . and you may never know how much business you lose because of those "anti-referrals."

Tips by Cindy:

- **Be intentional for them.** Don't waste the time of a potential client or business. Make sure that the match you are suggesting is one that you genuinely believe could be successful. Your name is on this connection!

CONCLUSION

It really is the little things that matter when creating lasting and positive relationships with your customers, employees, co-workers, clients, and vendors. And sometimes, as business people, we need to take a moment to step back and look at the bigger picture. Business is about relationships and taking the time to build a positive, honest, and trusting relationship for the future. When you think about it, *everyone* can be a customer. They may not be a direct customer to your business, but you never know who someone else is connected to.

When you treat everyone like a customer, your business and relationships will blossom. The driving force for my company is to create an outstanding customer experience that no one can top. And when you treat everyone like a customer, everyone in your life is going to feel the same over-the-top treatment. When you genuinely care for those around you, not only will you expand your potential client network, you will build loyalty and trust with all those around you.

And I get it, sometimes it's just hard. We all can find excuses for why we are not going out and building the relationships we need to have our businesses or professional lives grow. But trust me, if you are passionate about advancing your career, building strong, personal, and loyal relationships is key! You have to always be thinking, "Everyone is a potential customer," and treat everyone that way!

So what's stopping you? Are you willing to obsess to success? You have the tools, tricks, and tips. Grab your business cards, go out, and make those connections today!

ABOUT THE AUTHOR

Cindy Koebele started TitleSmart, Inc. in 2007, during the collapse of the housing bubble. Her intense focus on creating a positive customer experience turned TitleSmart into one of the Inc. 5000 Fastest-Growing Private Companies in America in 2014, 2015, 2016, and 2017. Employees and colleagues alike count on Cindy's frankness and generous nature. She's known for giving employees latitude to find their niche within her business.

In June 2015, Cindy was named Ernst & Young Entrepreneur of the Year for the Upper Midwest, further cementing her status as a powerhouse leader and entrepreneur. Cindy was the only female to be named Entrepreneur of the Year in her category in 2015.

Born to Be an Entrepreneur

Cindy brought a childhood passion for entrepreneurship to the title insurance industry when she began working in an administrative role for the production department of a title insurance company in the 1980s.

She quickly moved into closing. After several years in the industry, she realized there was an opportunity to bring a higher level of service to residential and corporate clients. A born observer of people, Cindy's curiosity, along with her many travels and studies of different cultures, contributes to her ability to find common ground with almost anyone. She uses this skill to read her customers and create customized interactions with them.

Children's Book Author

In addition to her work at TitleSmart, Cindy is the author of two children's books, *Puppa-na-wuppana: The Beagle with the Magical Nose*, and *Puppa-na-wuppana: Living the Puppa-na-Life*, based on the adventures of her family's curious beagle. She visits local schools and libraries to read her books and promote a love of reading in young kids.

Commitment to the Community

Cindy serves as the President of the Board of Directors for Spare Key, a nonprofit that provides housing grants to parents with seriously ill or critically injured children.

Visit **CindyKoebele.com**

OTHER BOOKS
BY CINDY KOEBELE

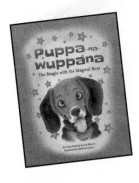

Puppa-na-wuppana,
The Beagle with the Magical Nose

Puppa-na-wuppana,
Living the Puppa-na-Life

Puppa-na-wuppana Plush Toy

Order at: Puppabooks.com